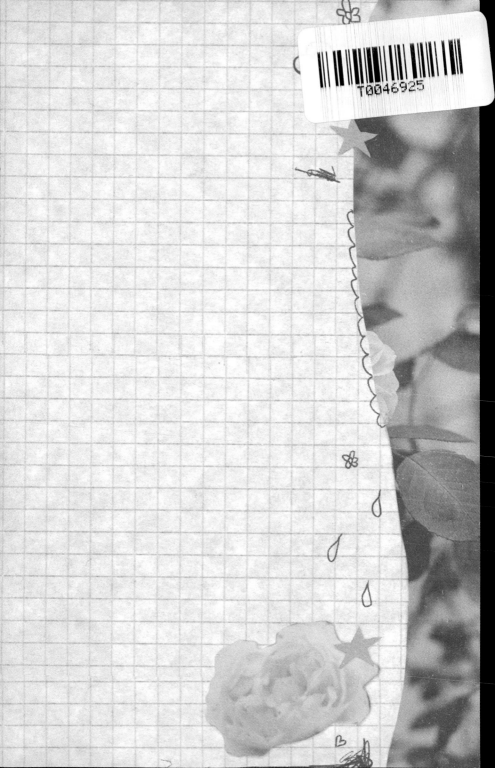

T0046925

"*The Surrender Theory* traverses the landscapes of love & grief with unwavering footsteps. These poems dive into vulnerability with their eyes wide open. I'm grateful to have spent time with this collection while navigating my own grief-broken heart. Thank you, Caitlin, for the reminder that it is worth it to live for the things we love."

— Sabrina Benaim, author of *Depression and Other Magic Tricks*

"Many have tried to describe the multitude of ways that grief can hold you, but none have come close to the way Caitlin transports you back into the feeling of its arms. *The Surrender Theory* is an engaging and accessible way to remember what it feels like to love. What it feels like to lose. The beauty in this collection lies in Caitlin's ability to detail her truth in a way that feels universal. We all have been touched by the feeling of yearning. This poetry will help you understand the depths of it. It will help you understand that you don't have to get lost in it."

— Ari B. Cofer, author of *Paper Girl and the Knives That Made Her*

"Conlon knows the essence of capturing an audience. Her signature voice is familiar and comforting, like she knows a part of you that even you have yet to discover. Anyone who has felt grief and the complexity of the human experience will confide in Conlon's work. She has the ability to see life through its clutter and she will show you that you can too."

— Zane Frederick, author of *i am tired of being a dandelion*

the surrender theory

poems

Caitlin Conlon

central
avenue
PUBLISHING

2022

Published by Central Avenue Publishing, an imprint of Central Avenue Marketing Ltd.
www.centralavenuepublishing.com

THE SURRENDER THEORY

Trade Paperback: 978-1-77168-261-9
Ebook: 978-1-77168-262-6

Published in Canada
Printed in United States of America

1. POETRY / General   2. POETRY / Women Authors

10 9 8 7 6 5 4 3 2 1

For Dolly

Content Warning: this book contains sensitive material related to death, grief, and mental health.

the surrender theory

THE SURRENDER THEORY

there isn't much that scares me more
than my own heart

a monster
       of tenderness.

I have an irrational fear that I'll wake to find it
perched at the
       foot of my bed
begging to be torn apart, consumed
in the name of compassion.
& that's incredibly terrifying
for a few different reasons but
mainly because I'd do it.

I've never needed an excuse
to sacrifice myself for love.
I'm a martyr for everything soft.

I confess to you: I'd bleed for anything
if it held me the right way.

I confess: I have.
                I have.

I CAN TELL IT'S AQUARIUS SEASON BECAUSE MY KNUCKLES ARE SPLITTING

What I thought was forever was just
last year. My body has attempted every
rebellion at least twice. Like ice in a
snowstorm, the future has solidified
on the doorknobs. It asks me for the key.

There's no way I'm making it out of here alive.

THE POET HAS A ONE-SIDED CONVERSATION WITH HER JOURNAL

Do you ever get the impression
that you're on the wrong side
of your own life?

I just mean that sometimes it feels like
a constant battle between wanting it
to feel the same, and knowing that it
shouldn't.

Okay, so I wrote myself out of the dark
but I can feel it creeping back in.

Is it too late to outrun my fate?

OBSERVATION

I don't know it's the last time which is, by nature,
what makes it a last time. When you can predict the
future every juncture
splinters
into smaller junctures,
last time after last time after last time. When you
don't, can't know, what awaits you, the moment just
is. It breathes. Looks around.

I look around. *Pitbulls and Parolees* plays on the
television, our conversation punctuated by barks and
howls. An off-white curtain separates her from
another patient, a patient I never see the face of. In an
emergency she'd be the first one out of the room.

I had to cut through a lobby, take an elevator, and
walk down a hallway to get here. I turned right into
the doorway. I will turn left to leave. If I write about
the setting it gives me an excuse to turn away from its
center. The catalyst, my grandmother.

She holds my hand, briefly, and doesn't sound like a
person that's known almost eighty Februarys, almost
eighty Valentine's Days. That's a lot of love, I want to
say, a lot of snow, but then I'd have to admit I'm not
listening as well as I should because I'm assuming
that there's endless time to say everything I need to
say.

And why shouldn't I? She's healthy, active. She goes
to the doctor. She knows who I am.

She asks about [redacted].
How was your date with [redacted]?
"We should look into getting you birth control."
I laugh. In my memory I slow this down, freeze
frame. I love her. In slow motion I love her fiercely.

Later I will regret spending so much time talking
about [redacted]. I will hate myself for describing in
detail the meal [redacted] cooked for us instead of
saying thank you. Thank you for every insignificant
thing. Thank you for leaving me notes on the kitchen
counter with chocolate whenever I go to bed sad.
Thank you for the singing toothbrushes and telling me
that my writing is beautiful. Even then, when it wasn't
quite beautiful. Just loud. At 19 I needed everyone to
share my bellyaches. At 19 I walk out of the room that
becomes our final private memory and think *what if
this is the last time* and promptly ignore it.

Look at her, sitting up with a pillow behind her.
Orange juice in a sealed cup on the side table.
This is not what an ending looks like, waving at me
from the doorway. Gown catching on a thin blanket. It
can't be. It isn't. I turn left. I keep going. I keep going
until I can breathe.

PANTOUM FOR WAITING ROOMS

& nobody ever tells you that life is full of mini-deaths,
or that // it never gets easier to erase your past into
memory. // Memory — little more than obsessive
remembering but we feed it like a habit, // until the
heart transcends the body & its tiresome hunger.

It never gets easier to erase your past into memory. //
When my grandmother died I watched a million little
deaths become a cloud. // Until the heart transcends
the body & its tiresome hunger // you cannot escape
the hands of it.

When my grandmother died I watched a million little
deaths become a cloud // & they hovered over her
body for warmth, mourning their penultimate death. //
You cannot escape the hands of it. // Every day
another part of me crawls into unnameable territory.

& they hovered over my body for warmth, mourning
their final death. // The doorway said "know, that god
hears prayers" so I became an atheist. // Every day
another part of me crawls into unnameable territory. //
Thank [ ] for that.

DOUBLE VISION

My grandmother's body
        was still warm and I was reckless enough to
call him mine. His hands on my bare waist like
electric paddles and I didn't care because I was
immortal. If death has taught me anything it's that I'm
alive and dangerously close to the boiling point. The
next day

my grandmother's body
        was cool and I drove to his apartment just to
unbutton a pair of jeans. I didn't tell him that I felt
like the Main Character of The Grief Story, that I
knew my body less than he did, but I repeated *I trust
you, I'm ready, I trust you, I'm ready* when what I
really meant was closer to *I could, I want to,* and even
this knowledge would only come to me once it was
over.

My grandmother
        wasn't a ghost yet and I allowed him to
become the entire sky above me. My whole life —
split open in every way imaginable. There isn't much
that I can recall in detail but I know he washed his
hands. I can smell the latex, picture the fresh razor
burn. And, of course, I remember the lights. How he
turned them off and snored and I thought *is this all
there is? Is this it? Am I even here at all?*

Then, all at once,
I knew.

A (hopefully) HELPFUL TIMELINE OF MY GRIEF

2017   2018   2019

←————————————————————————→

...etc   THE AFTERMATH   etc...

MY GRANDMOTHER DIES HOURS BEFORE VALENTINE'S DAY

MY FIRST BREAKUP, MORE CATASTROPHIC THAN IT SHOULD'VE BEEN DUE TO ITS PROXIMITY TO THE BIG GRIEF i am obsessed with the aftermath

i am obsessed with the aftermath

i am obsessed with the aftermath

i am obsessed with the aftermath

i am obsessed with the aftermath

i am obsessed with

the aftermath

i am obsessed with the aftermath

i am obsessed with the aftermath

i am obsessed with the aftermath

i am obsessed with the aftermath

THE AFTERMATH

I'm waist-deep in April
but my stomach is in February.
In the parking lot outside of my pharmacy
I stare at an orange bottle of antidepressants
that insurance no longer covers.
If my therapist were still my therapist
I'd say mindfulness isn't cutting it anymore.
The problems I blew into her tissues
seem unbearably simple, now.
Nobody was dead.
I'd yet to experience the romantic love I craved
so deeply, and therefore had never sat, helpless,
within its endless darknesses.
I gorged on happiness hours before its expiration date. Potential
stretched before me like a dinner table.
Life is magnificent just before it tries to kill you.

Mere weeks before graduating
out of my treatment program
I shared my illogical fear
of being abandoned in the center of my life,
hidden from anyone that could possibly understand me.

Some people, I divulged, are bigger than forgetting.
I don't think I'm one of those people.

CODED SIGNALS

You'll be happy to hear that I'm trying not to use the
word love as a placeholder for what I really want to
say STOP This is not because I suddenly know what
to say COMMA but because even in the privacy of
my own body I prioritize your grief STOP As if you'll
even know STOP As if you want me to STOP How's
this for a placeholder STOP I don't know what I
believe in anymore but I know it isn't god STOP Or
love STOP Or you

STOP

There I go   STOP   Tainting everything by writing
it down STOP   Even then I couldn't escape entirely
from the rabbit hole of *that* word STOP   And here
I am COMMA granting you immortality on a page
when the story is as simple as "you left"

STOP

I can't keep sitting here COMMA elbows deep in the
thought that this just wasn't supposed to work out for
us STOP

You can't keep blaming this on timing when the
minute hand is underneath your tongue STOP Was it
not enough that I let you rewrite my history STOP
Was it not enough STOP Was I not enough STOP

I MISS YOU STOP SO MUCH STOP AND I DON'T
KNOW STOP WHAT TO DO STOP

I STOP DO STOP NOT STOP KNOW STOP HOW
STOP TO STOP LET STOP THIS STOP

go

LIES

after Yena Sharma Purmasir

I did not know heartbreak at a young age / Intimacy
comes naturally to me / I'm the type of person that
leaves and doesn't look back / I've forgotten why it
hurts so much to be alone / Nothing reminds me of
him / I'm fluent in more than one language / I have
never thought at length about how I will die / I have
never met anybody that reminded me of a sunflower /
I always know exactly what to say / It has only ever
been like this / The possibility of a higher being has
never felt realistic / I have never used a Ouija board / I
have never tried to communicate with something that I
knew was dead / Depression does not prevent me
from taking care of myself / I will sit in the driveway,
alone, and have no idea what stops me from walking
inside / It is possible for me to feel safe when I am not
being loved / I believe that it will always ache this
terribly / I wrote you a letter and never sent it / I drove
home at dawn and did not think once, not even once,
about your mouth.

FIGURATIVELY SPEAKING

i feel like a papercut that never stops bleeding,
a rifle discharging into a thicket
named after your brother.

in my head we have more than a bedroom
and some unfinished letters to our legacy.
i rewrite our boring, unremarkable memories
and turn us into a fairytale.

the reality is that i still think of you as bandaid and ointment
when you're closer to emaciated animal
or beaten path to elsewhere.

this was never supposed to be a metaphor for anything.
i just wanted to love you. i tried so hard to do it right.

ROUTINE MAINTENANCE

Which grief can I live with today? I've barely been
awake five minutes when the question arrives,
tail tucked between its legs, waiting for an answer.

This is what I've learned
after months of meandering between melancholies:
it's easier to lick the wounds of a battered heart
than it is to raise someone from the dead.

LINGUISTICS

in a language that doesn't have the word 'love' I say,
"the receipt from the film we watched on our first date
is still tacked on my bulletin board." I say, "I bought
four red sweaters after you told me your favorite
color." I say, "it's been exactly two hundred and
twelve days since our last kiss." I say, "last week, in a
hotel room, the complimentary shampoo was the
same kind that you use." I say, "I walked around
smelling like you and nobody else cried over it." I say,
"yes, I'm still crying over it." I say, "the other day a
stranger's phone sang with the same noise you used
for your alarm and it took me all day to figure out
where I knew it from." I say, "I'm terrified of
someday not knowing where I knew it from." I say,
"every poem I've written lately is about the same
thing." I say, "I'd almost give up writing altogether if
it meant we could try again." I say "please," I say
"please," I say

"please"

TITLES FOR FUTURE BREAKUP POEMS

1. *Earth, Wind & Fire Wrote A Song About Your Birthday*
2. *It's September And I'm Feeling Sentimental About Your Liver*
3. *It's Nowhere Near September And Your Name Is Not A Song*
4. *WHY IS IT SO HARD TO CALL THIS WHAT IT WAS*
5. *Can I Call Someone "Mine" If They Never Understood Me?*
6. *If I Called...*
7. *If I Called Would You Remember The Words?*
8. *You Were My First Everything And I Want Them All Back*
9. *Everyone Likes Me Better When I'm Not Talking About You & I Don't Blame Them (Or You)*
10. *Do I Really Need To Write Another Poem Where We Break Up?*
11. *What If I Left Us Open To Interpretation?*
12. *I Think Of You On September 21st, And On Days That Are Not September 21st*
13. *I Think Of Regular, Ordinary Things, Throughout My Regular, Ordinary Life, And Sometimes You Arrive. Unannounced. I Don't Panic, Because Nothing Could Ever Make Me Miss Us More Than I Missed Us While We Were Still Together.*

ARE YOU LYING TO YOURSELF?

No, but I'm dishonest. No, but I'm forgetful. No, but I'm creating an emergency out of the way I don't recognize myself in the mirror. No, but I'm putting a period on the end of my adolescence and hoping that completes it. No, but I'm lying to everyone else. No, but maybe. No, but sometimes the absence is better than the truth. I say "no" because I'm too afraid of "yes." I repeat the same thing over and over, hoping it will distract you from seeing how little I know myself at all.

& that's the truth.
I don't know who I am anymore.

PAREIDOLIA

It's been over a year and I still look for him
in everything. A reflex I can't stop responding to.

I cling with blistered hands and bitter heart to any
story, any fiction, any song remotely like ours, as if
it'll give our conclusion meaning.
Or, at the very least, a name I can call out
when I'm fading away.

Even in make-believe kitchens that were never written to hold his
body, his fingerprints decorate the sugar jar.

Every time I confuse us with adults in love
I move further away from the reality
of whatever we were.

I REENACT "THE LAST FIVE YEARS" IN MY KITCHEN INSTEAD OF GOING TO THERAPY

I close my eyes and imagine the scenario
which never changes. My ex
has come to see the show not knowing
I'm playing the lead. I am the grand surprise,
the knife in his evening, a smile dripping with
promises quickly retracted. For an hour
and sixteen minutes my name is Cathy Hiatt.

Singing to my chipped kitchen cabinets
is the only release I have from these endless days
of pushing through windows.
Props line the countertops, ready to supplement
choreography I've memorized, blending fiction
and reality into an edible pulp.

It's for the art, I tell myself backstage, shaking in the
living room, tears like the Hudson. *You're acting, and
it's for the art, and you're on stage, and this is real
life, so don't mess up, girl. You auditioned for this
role. You fit it so perfectly.*

Always it comes down to both of us, Cathy and
Caitlin, sitting on linoleum
after the curtain's been drawn shut, wondering
how he could've given up so easily.
Contemplating the words we should've said
instead of written into a song, or poem.
And then there's him, moving on,

reinventing the world with little more than a pen.

We weren't asking to be rescued.
No, we just wanted to be the type of girl
he'd come home to.
At the center of our heartbreak is a summer day
set to melody, ten minutes of forevers,
climbing, climbing, climbing
until there's nowhere left but

down.

No matter our role in the undoing
he didn't have to leave like that.

YOU COOKED FOR ME

once, in the time that we were together. Pasta.
Vegetarian.

I leaned against your doorway, not yet comfortable
in any place that belonged to you, and said
how touched I was that you'd listened to my nervous
babble on our first date. *No meat, but dairy is fine.*

It felt like the kindest thing anyone had ever done
for me — mixing handmade pesto in a white bowl.
Clearing away a stack of unopened mail from a stool
so I could sit and watch the steam rise.

In retrospect I can see that you gave me very little
and I tried to build an entire future with it.

You must understand, I had never been remembered
like that, before.

With purpose. Without begging for it.

I took what I was offered and ran.

NICK CARRAWAY WAKES IN THE MIDDLE OF THE NIGHT, AND REACHES FOR A PEN

I wonder how this would've played out
if you'd known all along that I was going
to write about it. If you'd known my intention
was to expose the green light as metaphor, trip
over the white silk curtains,
would you have said my name any differently?

Ours was a story that begged for clarity.
While love was sleeping it was me that ripped
away the sheets and identified it as obsession.
I refuse to apologize for honesty even if all
it's left me with are ghosts. Does it bring you back?
No. Does it accurately depict how much
I cared for you? Also no.

The signs that I should've noticed sooner have
followed me and I welcome their stare, so much
like yours, seeing a certain reliability in me
and never bothering to name it. So maybe I'm
too late. Maybe life is little more than a car crash or a
sweltering city but dammit, I loved you so much that I
made you the hero of the story rather than the fool.
I wrote you face-down in the pool and rowing into
the past, slow enough for me to catch the wake of
you, lapping against my chest like a grateful animal
or a current of grief.

You were the death of an ideal I'd never tasted but

dreamt of swimming across. I rue the hours I wasted
holding my breath for a fantasy. This was never
going to end the way I wanted it to.
I knew this, and still tried to give you an ending
worthy of history.

You died for love, like you'd always wanted.
Crimson enveloping your body in a cloud of
gunpowder and chlorine. Later,
Judgment and I would stand over your possessions
remembering parties thrown for a future that could
never be. A future that language couldn't have
accommodated.

Nowadays I don't know what to do with my hands.
I write. I say your name over and over
until it isn't a word. I sit outside and weep
into the daisies until memory becomes less of a
burden
and more of a fact. At the end of the day you are still
gone and I am still a storyteller, sitting on a chair
you will never touch, staring into an abyss
that remains silent despite the hole I have torn into it
with my suffering. Accompanied only by the blue
jays, and their songs like tender mourning.

i have
friends
that will
never hear me
say your name

FIELD NOTES

ok, so here's what i know. i have to keep talking
because the silence is underwhelming.

i feel like a busy intersection of
green stop signs.

sometimes the only place i can bear to leave us
is at the beginning.

BELATED QUESTIONS

there are at least a million ways to set fire to
something but only one good way to put it out. so
maybe i smothered us. can you forgive me for wanting
this so badly that i ruined the couch cushions? i used
to daydream about running into you in public, because
i needed you to see how much better i was doing but,
looking back, maybe i just wanted assurance that
you're still alive. how do i talk about all of that
without making it seem like i'm still obsessed with
you? is it healthy to care, distantly, and with no stake
in the situation, for the person i knew you were going
to be? in any burning building there are at least two
exits but when everything's red how are you supposed
to read the signs? i'm asking too many questions
again, i know. this doesn't seem like my story to tell
anymore but what was this situation if it wasn't mine?
even now, there are veins of you stretching away from
my own. memories i don't want to bury because of the
person i would kill in the process. she was so eager,
unafraid of what love could do to her. what it did. if i
could give you one last thing it would be this: i no
longer think of you with yearning, only curiosity.

NEW VOICEMAIL
9:02 AM
22 SECONDS

meet me at the

[inaudible]

The wet dog of desire jumps into my bed and I let it.

I'll sleep next to anything if it means I won't be alone.

WHERE MY GRANDMOTHER HIDES

I find her at the bottom of every glass I drink from.
It's always the same — I'll tip my head back for one
final, blissful gulp, and then find her staring back at
me from the emptiness. She is as I remember her;
alive. Curly dyed-blonde hair rustles around flushed
skin as I adjust the cup for a better look. An avalanche
of words threatens to burst out of my mouth and I
restrain them in my throat. I want to ask if she's still
proud of me, apologize for the way I abandoned my
feet after she left, but nothing sounds like what needs
to be said. So we stare, thoughtfully, condensation
surrounding us, a damp circle of everything we
would've shared if we'd recognized our last
conversation for what it was. White-knuckled grip
eventually fades into understanding, unclenching.
My grandmother only exists in the remnants
of thirst long enough for me to miss her,
which is to say, not long. Sometimes
we say goodbye to each other as
though it is a shared name. I call
it out to her almost violently
as she dissipates into
nothing.

PERSONAL BELIEFS

My grandmother speaks to me through
pennies discarded on cement.
The truth is not the truth until you say it
to the first thing you survived.
Joy is difficult to obtain
when you most require it.
If my depression answers to anything
it isn't my reflection.
You can lose things
while holding onto them.
The symphony of childhood sounds best
when played in reverse.
Forgiveness is not enough if

_____.

I RUINED
LOVE
BY GIVING IT
A NAME

ECHO

in the attic of my adolescence
pigeons never stop cooing. baby
blankets and cotton candy are used
for insulation. i whisper your name into
the dark and it never thinks to come back.

THE RED ROOM

We walked into the red room together,
but did not walk out of it at the same time.
The red room pulsated around us, like the walls
of a hungry stomach.
& in the red room we held hands &
did not call it anything. & if you listen closely,
the red room still sounds like our small talk.
The red room still sounds like the stories I told
thinking they would make me seem
cool, like a girl that could learn how to give
a good kiss. & I visited the red room
with a man I could adore & hated
that the ghost of you was still lingering, trailing
your fingers along the walls as if it could
shrink the foundation, envelop me. & sometimes
I think part of me will always be in the red room
because the red room is where I realized that I was
a person worthy of love.
& now the red room is the red room
& I am loved but not by you & that is what I want.
The first time I ever left the red room
I thought you were going to save me from a life
of disappointment. The last time I left the red room
I felt lucky to have outlasted
what you put me through.
& I watched out of the corner of my eye
as the red room absorbed everything we ever did
inside of it, which still wasn't enough.

& then the red room opened the windows.

& the red room let it go.

SPEED DATING IN THE TWENTY-FIRST CENTURY, OR A LIST OF THINGS YOU SHOULD KNOW ABOUT ME THAT REQUIRE A LEVEL OF URGENCY

I recycle because it makes me feel good about myself/
I take regifting seriously/ I smile when uncomfortable/
I can't parallel park/ I keep receipts to remember
where I've been/ I've never been tested for allergies/ I
have been in love twice/ I only knew what that meant
once/ I was kissed for the first time in the Buffalo
Science Museum and began to associate affection
with artifacts/ I want to be reborn as an airport gift
shop or rest stop/ I am enchanted by the liminal/ I was
once told that nobody would ever love me because
being in my presence was like walking on thin ice/ I
forget details but remember feelings/ I think you're
probably going to leave/ I think you're probably going
to leave/ I think you're *probably* going to *leave*/ And
you should know that I stay/ And you should know
that I'm capable of terrible, awful things/ And most
importantly you should know that

I'm not ashamed of my heart anymore

JOY, IN ONE ACT

I didn't expect to confront joy
for the first time in fourteen months
from the seat of a parked car
but I also didn't expect to be chased around
a waiting room by grief, so maybe
what I'm trying to say is that I never know
where or when certain feelings will find me,
I just know how to describe it when they do.

What I *can* tell you about joy
is that it has round reading glasses
and prefers Halloween to Christmas.
Drums on the steering wheel
to the classic rock station and
orders fried pickles from the Tully's appetizer menu.
Tells me a secret and trusts me to hold it tight.
Kissed me last night under the glow of a streetlamp
and made me question why I kept it for so long
at arm's length.

My own body a barrier, my own hands
obstructing the view.

OURS, AWAY

i haven't done this in a while
so please forgive anything that may fall
out of my mouth when i'm touching you.
the firework show making an open field of my chest.
your face, the spark.

later i'll shower in the light of a tangerine candle,
the shadow flames flickering against curtain
akin to your tongue on the inside of my thigh.
it's been a long time since i've felt present in this
body.

i wipe steam away from the mirror
and fixate on the hand stretched in front of me
like a beacon. it's shaking. i haven't completely
forgotten how to want something this badly.

excuse all the delicate pageantry, the melodrama,
how i sighed loudly into your chest when we had
to say goodbye.

you make me want to believe in love again.

ERASURE OF "I NEED YOU" BY AMERICA

We   laugh
And
carry on And make the best of

                  the rain.
                  I need you,
you know

I need you.

NESTING DOLL

My grandmother's death is a big grief — the size of,
maybe, a medicine ball. Anything bigger than that
is no longer grief, it is hopelessness, which is
generally much worse. Nobody talks about it, it being
hopelessness, without lying at least a little bit. I do not
want to lie, anymore. Lying is a plum-sized grief.
When I was younger I treated truth carelessly and
cannot tell you why, only that the guilt never tasted
quite as bitter as it should have. Guilt is a watermelon-
sized grief. Premature forgiveness is a peach.
There is something terribly fitting about eating loss
when you're able to.
I have not always been able to.
Misplacing love for the first time was a wad of taffy
as big as my head. I crawled away with a cavity
on my canine but at least I crawled away.
The trick is to stop believing you will come away
unscathed and, instead, prepare for the inevitability
of upheaval. One time my grandmother asked me
if she was the reason that I was always so sad
and I told her the truth, which was that I don't know
why I'm always so sad. What I should've said, what
she probably needed to hear, was *you are the opposite
of what is misprinted in my foundation,* but I've never
really been one for saying the right thing at the correct
time, which, of course, is why I write, why I'm here
at all, meditating on grief, trying to say something that
sounds nicer than *I would like you to come home, now.*

I would like you to take your shoes off by the coat rack and leave me notes on the kitchen counter, brag about me to your friends as I turn into a strawberry, take me to terrible matinee comedies and pretend we both hated them. I promise that, if you do, I'll stop talking to loose change on the sidewalk, poking at the birth mark on my chest that isn't there anymore, eating the flowers we once planted so carefully by the big tree. Dolly, they taste so sweet, and fresh. Like a place I could finally be happy in.

THE DEPRESSION NOTES

When the hurt comes I crawl quietly
into his belly
and contort my body into a circle,
suck oxygen in through a straw poking out
of his mouth.

I wait until it's safe to return to myself,
wait hours longer than that,
and then slip back into the present
as a river will fade
into a larger river.

Depression is a broad and
        twisted sort of desperation.
A waiting room television that never
shuts off, though I have tried.
        Reaching with the best parts of me
        toward joy, wondering if joy can
        see how my best parts tremble
like the ears of a rabbit.

The years I've lost to my mind
haunt me like a bad memory.
I'm stuck inside the throat
of forgetfulness.
(I'm still naming my mistakes
after cities I've cried in.)

When you take a blade
to your past, where do you go
to bury the hatchet?

How do you forgive your name
for being your name?

& whenever I talk about It
I feel dirty, not *because*
I have It but because I'm
convinced that I'm a liar.
I google imposter syndrome
and hide behind my advocacy
for better representation. Say
"MENTAL ILLNESS DOES
NOT MAKE ME WEAK"
while feeling like a fraud,
parading my illness around
in a flashy cape, hoping maybe,
just maybe, somebody will
see it and feel lightened by
validation rather than buried.

it's like, there's a transparent layer between
my actual self and my physical body.
i can see myself moving through the world
but i'm also separate. watching from
behind the glass. nothing is interesting.
it takes all of my energy to move from the bedroom
to the kitchen and get something to eat.
then i need to go back to the bedroom and take a nap
before i can do anything else. or, that's what i want to
do. but then anxiety wakes up and i can't fall asleep.
why am i wasting my day? do you think you have
enough time left in your short life to waste your day?
so i lie there, awake, scrolling through my phone,
because apparently that counts as not wasting the day.
eventually he comes in and kisses my face,
and has me take a walk to clear my head.
so i find myself kicking leaves away from my feet
during a depressive episode, counting reasons
to stay alive.
1.   i am already alive.
2.   i don't think it's always this difficult to breathe.
3.   i have so much love in my life and
i am becoming somebody i don't mind seeing
in the mirror.
4.   i don't want to die anymore. my thoughts trick me
     sometimes but i don't want to die anymore. i don't
     want to die anymore. i don't want to die anymore.

.

the sadness feels like a weighted sweater
pushing me further and further into myself.

not every day.
but enough of them.

Depression has so many faces.
And yet, somehow, I am still
every single one of them.

SO, WHAT CAN YOU REMEMBER?

Not much, which makes me greedy for anything
that sounds like it could belong to my
body.

I hold the past in a handkerchief and wash it after
every touch, like if I linger with the memory for too
long

it'll make me sick. When I put on my grandmother's
rain coat for the first time after she died, I shoved
hands into

the pockets and unearthed two balled-up tissues of
surrender. I looked at them until they glowed and then
held

the feeling to my chest. I remember that, at least. Not
the feeling, but my chest. I think that if I ever wander
into

understanding — full and untethered understanding —
I'll have to sit down for a couple of years. I'd rather
be forgetful

than know exactly what I've lost.

CLAIRVOYANCE

At eight years old I was psychic. Pressed fingers to
every living thing and gave it a future. I am my own
best historian because when I change the details it
goes unnoticed. At eight years old I was psychic / NO
/ I plucked leaves from the oak tree in my front yard
and hid them in my cheeks, just to see if this would
make the world shatter, and if it did, it waited many
years, examining my heels, before striking. The
moons between me and my formative experiences
race past my body like a searchlight that never lands
on anything living. At eight years old I was psychic /
NO / I killed the plant / NO / I ran away from home
on a plastic rowboat that my grandmother and I raced
down the creek behind our house. More proof that I'm
a historian — everyone in my poems has died. At
eight years old I was psychic / NO / I spit out the
leaves / NO / I planned my escape / NO / I bit into a
scarlet apple and left shards of bone buried in its flesh.
My dead grandmother scooped the apple and baby bits
into a plastic bag so it would fit the Tooth Fairy's
requirements for payment. See? I was raised like this,
saving everything under my pillow. I was taught that
following the rules would get me what I wanted. At
eight years old I thought I was psychic / NO / I
fabricated an oak tree / NO / the creekbeds dried up /
NO / I sacrificed my body for a lie / NO / NO! / I just
wanted to be good. All along I just wanted to be good.
At eight years old I was psychic. I held my

grandmother's arm and told her about the decades of serendipity she had to look forward to. I gave her a future longer than she was given. I gave her a future that outlived my own and then I wrote it down.

NUMB RECOLLECTIONS

I was awake when they took my wisdom teeth.
The novocaine shots were enough to cry over but I
remember the sound more vividly than the hurt itself.
That terrible cracking of bone into confetti excavated

from my mouth like pieces of ancient pottery. Bloody
shards that the dentist allowed me to hold, cradle
gently in dubious hands. This former bite. This
shattered vase overflowing with history. Something

that could've lived forever if I'd just left it alone. But
I suppose that's the point — I'd rather remove all
signs of growth than bargain with maybe. My
grandmother wanted to watch them work so she sat

beside me throughout the procedure. I studied her face
as they operated, how it contorted and made me feel
throbbing that wasn't there. Days later I would go to
Denny's with friends and only be able to eat oatmeal

and pancakes. I liked having an excuse to eat softly.
Liked being taken care of, adored watching television
in bed and accomplishing absolutely nothing. I could
mourn the loss of myself in peace. Back then every

summer day was a coughing fit, which made the chest
ache in that particular way you can never recount
accurately. I spent them with tongue flitting across
gums, relearning the boundaries of speech, taste,

known world. On the drive home, numb and
weightless, I sang *I can't feel my face when I'm with
you* and laughed and laughed. I couldn't feel anything.

I couldn't feel anything at all.

you are no
longer a
trait i
use to describe
myself with

YOU WILL NEVER BE ABLE TO BURY
THE PERSON YOU WERE WHEN YOU
LOVED THEM

ANXIETY AS INHERITANCE
after Søren Kierkegaard

Before sin there was the apple,
      before the apple there was anxiety.
The threat of unutterable tragedy hung
      scarlet, burning, exodus.
Like a matchstick in the hand of
      death, an offering without language.
If disorder predates ancestral sin
      then maybe apprehension is god-like.
Anxious comes from the Latin
      anxius, from *angere*, to choke.
A wedge of fruit caught in the
      throat, unforgiving and shameful.
My bare body, forced
      to accept the unpredictable.

YOU SAY ACNE

and I hear skin for miles, crimson enough
to rival ripe berries, warm enough to kiss.
When I drag fingers across my face they rest
instinctually on the areas I've made mountains of.
Tissue in hand because I'm tender; press too hard
and I'll burst.

At the age of 12 cruelty does not know its own voice.
When they pointed at my cheeks and called them
gross I thought it honesty rather than shame.
The mirror spoke to me through running water, bars of
soap slipping into a sink, ads claiming face masks
and foundations are key to loving the skin you're in.
"The skin you're in." As if it's unattached to the self,
destined for abandonment. As if what I've grown is
just draped over the edges of *inner beauty*.
As if I'm not everything I've ever created
and then some.

It's not too late to claim it so I will.
It's all mine; the stained cloth pressed against chin.
This inflamed face. The scars and their memories.

My planet and all its cratered moons
are spinning in a solar system
that's so far away.

ODE TO DRY SHAMPOO

Diligent can of oil-absorbing magic.
Beauty product must-have go-to.
Keeper of hair-care secrets
and last night's misadventures,
I bow down to your grease-fighting abilities
in the name of social acceptance.

Silver cloud composed of linings
I'd call you a miracle if I could pronounce
your ingredients.
The way you nestle into my scalp
and tango with my purple comb could put any dancer
to shame.
Your patience with my body has not gone unnoticed.

It's funny,   how people want to understand your mental
illness until you exhibit undesirable symptoms.
It's all *let me know if you need anything* until you run
out of energy to take care of yourself.
The trash bag sits by the door. The bedsheets grow
heavy. Then *lazy* enters the conversation
and where can you go from that?

Sometimes when you're depressed you can't shower.
By you I mean I, and by can't I mean what's the point
of being good to your body if your body hasn't been
good to you? I mean all I want to do is sleep. When
I'm dreaming I don't have to think. To bring soap to

skin and scrub existential dread away, watch the drain
swallow me up, is risky and exhausting. I swear it is.
I swear it is.

Dry Shampoo
I'm trying my hardest even though doing so puts you
out of a job.
Dry Shampoo
I'm supposed to feel guilty when I lift your cap,
press your nozzle.
I just want to leave the house without worrying
that everyone will know how utterly disgusting I feel.
Yes, I know it's disgusting.
I know it isn't healthy.
Stop acting like I'm ignorant to my faults when you
have the privilege of stepping away from this monster
I sustain. It's a terrible beast, my brain.
If you haven't known depression's hot breath on your
neck I suppose it wouldn't make sense. Sympathy
always draws a line somewhere,
often where it's most needed.

Dry Shampoo
in a world that will only value me
if my self-destruction is hidden, you comfort me.
You never pass judgment.
You acknowledge me when I come to you,
crusty-eyed and desperate for help.

You do something about it.

EN ROUTE TO THE BUS STATION

it's silent in the car, apart from the jazz music drifting
out of his speakers. his red monte carlo,
the one he's named cherry; i've been trying very hard
to remember everything he says to me.

he holds my hand as though it's an extension of the
steering wheel and i know that even though we
haven't said it, we already miss each other. isn't that
ironic? i've spent lifetimes yearning for the person i
knew he would be and now, though i've shared a
summer of exhales with his skin and touched the
dreams he breathes into my bedspread, i still miss
him. this want is unrelenting. i wonder if maybe that's
all love is—
—constantly dreading the next collective moment of
departure, fearing anything that could complicate
returning.

if i wanted to puncture this moment i would
remind the saxophones and trumpets that new york
city doesn't have anything on him, but that's pretty
cheesy and i think i would probably cry if i had to say
it out loud, so i don't.

instead, i bring his wrist to my mouth and hum against
it so he'll know that i'm still here.

for the next eighteen minutes i will still be here, with

him, and cherry, and the sound of the late august night
squeezing itself through his cracked window, begging
to be included.

buffalo's city lights reflect on the niagara river like
submerged lanterns and i count the number of seconds
between my *i love you* and his response.

time is not always long enough to mention.

unless it's ours.

SAYING YOUR NAMES

after Richard Siken

Your name like vital organs carried inside of me.
Your name like forgiveness. Your name like my eight
year old self asking for god's advice in the form of
flickering streetlamps. One flicker for no. Two for
"I'm listening." Your name like a candy wrapper
unfolded in the library. Your name like sheets
stretched taut over mattress corners. Your name like a
siren, spiraling into emergency. Your name like knee-
deep saltwater biting into ankle blisters. Your name
like the arrival section of an airport. Your name like
missed connection boards. Your name like allegory
worth repeating. Your name like spontaneity. Your
name like used books with margin notes. Your name
like a choir. A band. A song. Your name like my
name. Like something I can't remember ever learning,
just blinking into existence knowing.

THE ARTIST PAINTS A FAVORABLE PORTRAIT OF JACK TORRANCE

I don't include a bottle and this is a gift to both of us.
You can comfortably hang the finished product in the
hallway with pride, even if it will soon turn to ash
in your palms. This is a kinder version of the story,
where you pretend the sickness has passed and I
choose to believe it. Fear is unspoken, the hedges
asleep, the mallet of your rage is a tool and not a
weapon.

The red paint yields more bottom of the pan than any
other color and still the strokes don't stop. Here I take
care to cover up the child you loved, but not enough to
admit your shortcomings. A flat wash over the cheap
kitchen glasses you mixed your gin into before
grabbing the car keys. I say that this will require time
to paint accurately and you smile at me with all of
your teeth — not quite a wolf, but a caricature of one.
Anyone that didn't know better would love the way
it catches the light.

The ballet of your life may end with a drink, Jack, but
you'll never be able to run from the taste. For years
you've staggered to churches just wanting a place to
bow your head. You've spent eternities studying the
flight patterns of sobriety and cannot reach a hand out
for it to land. It may be easy to romanticize, but that
doesn't mean your life has been romantic. Only that
addiction runs through me like memory and every

time I drink I wonder if this will be the one that starts the cycle over again.

If you ask the canvas, depression is a window slamming shut and remaining there, light leaking through the glass. If you ask the artist, it's a bird that sings only when it feels cowardly. A choir of faceless clocks screaming about wasted time.

I lay the portrait out to dry once I can no longer bear to handle it and don't bother to sign my name.

Everything I have ever created is a love letter to my identity.

WENDY TORRANCE PRACTICES REVISIONIST HISTORY

and the only story she cares to edit is that of her son.
Her beautiful boy. While he sleeps, she slips quietly
into his bedroom and seizes memories by the fistful,
unrooting the trauma, not realizing that she's severing
the bond between acceptance and closure. As she
works she can feel her late husband's spirit, freshly
unhaunted, pull off his hands and place them in her
lap, as if to say "These were heavy and I kept them
anyway. These were heavy and I never said so. These
were heavy but please know that my last words were
remember how much I love you and I didn't trip over
them." Wendy believes him, but that doesn't mean she
forgives his sins. If truth is a pair of hands then grief
is burying them without ceremony. The ritual is in the
act of admitting her shortcomings, in planting flowers
to cover the stench of departure and telling her son
that she just wanted something colorful to look at.
Wendy lights a cigarette in her bedroom, the smoke
forming an outline of a future cloudy and
untouchable. If she leans in close enough, she can
almost imagine it into something real.

SHAME LINEAGE

if i've learned anything about shame it's that when
you pass it down to your children they have no
choice but to carry it   tend to a deep
undeniable sadness   they are unable
          to name

You Must Accept
That The Violence
Of Your Past
Was Senseless
And Unearned

CALL ME NARCISSUS

It's almost summer so I pour one out for you. Out of
the second story window and onto the sidewalk
below, where it stares back up at me like a mirror.

I watch it for hours, in your honor.
Bystanders step on its shadow, a pitbull
takes a cursory sniff.
We've reversed roles: you are the mess
and I'm watching you dry.

Recently my father moved into your neighborhood
and, hoping for a reference point, I searched for your
street, before realizing I can no longer remember its
name.

The myths I told myself to keep you alive
are slowly becoming obsolete without anyone
to repeat them.

Time is erasing you without so much as an echo to
commemorate it.

it's easier to think of my life as one big epic poem
rather than a series of events that thrust me into
creativity as a means of survival. It's easier to think of
my life As one big epic poem rather than a series of
events that thrust me into creativity as a Means of
survival. it'S easier to think of my life as one big epic
poem raTher than a series of events that thrust me
into creativIty as a means of survival. it's easier to
think of my life as one big epic poem rather than a
series of events that thrust me into creativity as a
means of survivaL. it's easier to think of my life as one
big epic poem rather than a series of events that thrust
me into creativity as a means of survivaL. it's easier
to think of my life As one big epic poem rather than a
series of events that thrust me into creativity as a
means of survival. it's easier to think of my life as one
big epic poem rather than a series of events that thrust
me into creativity as a means of survivaL. it's easier
to think of my life as one bIg epic poem rather than a
series of events that thrust me into creatiVity as a
mEans of survival. it's easier to think of my life as one
big epic poem rather than a series of events that thrust
me into creativity as a means of survival. it's easier to
think of my life as one big epic poem rather than a
series of events that thrust me into creativity as a
means of survival. it's easier to think of my life as one
big epic poem rather than a series of events that thrust
me into creativity as a means of survival. it's easier to

THE ANXIETY SPEAKS
after Jeanann Verlee

I give you the gift of fortune telling and
        you repay me with this?
        Spit from a trembling mouth and
an open box to climb into?
        When the person sharing your bed realizes
I've been pulling the strings
maybe then you'll see how badly you need me.
        Lazy. Depression-ridden.
        Full of holes where your stomach acid has
made
        a fist, bones crafted by unkind
and shabby hands, mouth bloody, wet. Without me
you would've talked yourself into the
        good graces of loneliness and buried yourself
in its
        yard after one good meal.
I raise your lows. I make you whole.
I am the reason
        your heart curls up into a ball
        when the light disappears. I am the tears that
rupture
your eyes when you
        attempt to defend yourself. The reason you're
always waiting,
        debating, wondering if this
        is the right time to speak. It isn't, you thick-
tongued and
uncoordinated babbler. You never

know what to say and I stop you from saying it
anyway.
I've saved you from suffocating on
embarrassment too many times to count.
When I pull at your throat
or sit on your chest, know it's out of love.
I belong here. Just try one day
absent of my wrists. You'll beg me to save you
from the weight of your
own body before I've even packed my bags.

1:04 PM

Underneath the floorboards, buried with the sound of
your singing voice, I have finally laid the past to rest.

3:18 AM

sometimes i rip up all the floorboards
and still can't remember
how you said my name.

DOLLY CRIES DURING THE MOVIE

I'm thirteen and know my heart like running water
but not like a thing that carries you past danger.
Meryl Streep doesn't get out of the car
and I hate her for it. I hate her for choosing the bridge
over what's swimming underneath. The scene in
question is hot and suffocating — rain sliding down
windows like sweat on a bare neck, forming an
undrinkable puddle. My grandmother would joke that
she wished she'd married for money. Told me in
detail about dreams where our house became a
mansion and we finally had enough rooms for our
lonely. Clint Eastwood looks past the camera
and we sniffle into elbows that have seen different
mouths. Lately I've wondered about the kind of grief
only stories can revive. The kind of opening credits
that can rewrite your own folklore.
Even now the film is beautiful, despite these older
eyes and my dark apartment with no dining table
or chair for the piano. I can tell you why I cried
but not why she stayed.
The tears on her ancient cheeks were so susceptible
to the southwestern breeze, like an old woman's ashes
searching for a resting place, rich enough to bloom.

SELECTIVE ATTENTION

You are getting very sleepy. You are relaxing your
muscles one by one. You are my grandmother, trying
to quit smoking, and you are her future granddaughter,
visualizing an event she knows little about. You are
my grandmother visiting a hypnotist. You are the
hypnotist and the walls around them. You are telling
time in a room where minutes unfold like glue. You
are on the end of a very long chain, swinging freely in
the sunlight. You are unsure as to whether Hollywood
gets anything right. You are my grandmother's lungs,
accustomed to fire. You are undressing beneath a
pseudo-microscope. You are a storyteller and that
makes you a believer. You are a storyteller and that
makes you an inventor. You are inventing a memory
of my grandmother because they no longer occur
organically. You are building a universe where
everything you love is immortal. You are dangerous.
You are my grandmother leaving the hypnotist
with no desire for cigarettes. You are watching her leave
from the windows. You are here until the very end, as
any good storyteller is. You are not a very good
storyteller but someday you could be. You are waking
up, slowly. You are wondering how everything can
change so quickly, so entirely. You are the story and
everything around the story.

You are still you.
You are still.
You are.

PENELOPE

It's with fingertips tangled in crimson thread
that I begin to wonder

if perhaps I've been too gentle with the men I have
loved. Perhaps the waiting,

the solitude, the undeniable yearning, has been less
about holding people accountable

and more about testing my limits for sport.
I have always needed to prove myself to myself.

I decide that I am not a worthy lover if I don't spend
every waking hour unwinding my heart,

under the assumption that someday I'll
be held again and this labor

will not have been for nothing. If I stop,
even to rest my eyes,

then I deserve all the tangled nets and sea glass
that wash up onto the beach before me.

Sacrifice makes sense to me.
How else do you explain the countless bodies

I have turned away? The tired nature of the loom
that has become my paradox?

The songs I refuse to let any muse sing for me?
Shroud from a wounded tapestry tumbles lightly

over my hands as I work, like your hair would in the
rosy-fingered mornings before the storm.

Everything I remember reflects how I have loved you
which is entirely too much for what was given in

return. Is this too soft? If I can bite my tongue without
breaking my teeth is that too soft? If I can turn away

from the solace of real company while embracing the
ghost of your touch is that too soft? I look through

the window, to the night shimmering quietly, and am
reminded of a curtain thick with steam.

The way it sticks to itself as it wavers. It's lonely to be
in love. Nobody will ever know exactly how you feel.

It's even lonelier to love longer than you deserve to
but how do I know what I deserve if my story

is only ever told as addendum to yours? O, how I
could've had it all! Somebody that would listen

when I asked them to stay! I can't explain why I
continue this neverending pilgrimage into uncharted

waters. There are things that I will never be able to tell
you about grief but I have made peace with them.

I have invited them to watch me weave deception
into our timeline and they applaud me, praise

my courage, tell me *of course, of course he will want
who you've become,* which isn't a lie because

I believe it. Belief is critical to those that have
experienced loss. For example, I believe that this life

as an undoer is temporary. I believe that the gods are
not as smart as they think they are. I believe that

nestled deep in my throat there is a part of me that
will eternally, frantically, search for you

in every tide that devours our beaches. A part that
knots seaweed into ropes and unfurls them into the

great abyss. It's only once dawn greets my skin, as she
always does, sympathetically, that I can find

enough restraint to crawl into cool sheets
and accept the hours I have lost to remembering you,

placing my hands, vacant and worn, on the table
beside me. The loose threads from a history

not worth writing pool around my bed like a raft.
One of these days, I swear,

there will be nothing left to unravel for you.

VICTOR

it's june and i'm not sure i remember how to be kind.

consider starfish; without blood, brain, or opposable
finger they can recreate what's been taken from them.
what i'm trying to say is that i regrow tenderness
like a limb. i can't help it.

love asked me not to wait for it, so i did.

there are a lot of things i've learned since you left,
like, i won't die because of your choice to run. your
absence isn't brave enough to demolish all of this soft.

i'll likely never stop wondering whether or not you're
alive, which isn't nearly as terrible as it sounds.

i could be left with nothing at all, mere crumbs
from such a brief yet monumental era of my life.
i could probably still miss you in the same way
if i wanted to, but i don't want to.

language has muddied everything i've ever written for
you which, as you know, is a lot and
there are some things that i'd like to make clear.

i regret the way i treated you, when we began to
imagine different futures. i've questioned what we
could've been

if it weren't for my hands. at the core of it
this is meant to be an apology, for what i said to you
while grieving.

i did not know, yet, that i could be ugly without also
being cruel.

FINAL WISHES FOR EX LOVES

I wish them cool breezes on hiking days and shoes
that last longer than expected. An apartment with two
bedrooms and a kitchen full of food. I wish them
decent seats at every movie theater and used book
stores with reasonable prices. I wish them healthy
relationships with their parents and brothers. That
the radio occasionally plays a song worth turning up
the volume for. No wasps, no hornets, only bees and
flowering gardens. I wish them rainy evenings, ideal
for dreaming. I wish that they never have to read
another poem that makes them feel like a monster.
That they never kiss another writer. Forgiveness.
Growth. I wish them endless summers and short
winters. Girls that say their name like it's breakable. I
wish them a love that makes them marvel. A life
without me. Full, and meaningful. I wish them
happiness. I wish it in every shade of color there is.

IN DEFENSE OF THE BREAKUP POEMS

I know there were too many / I know they were
brought to life long after they should've been / but
you must see how they still throw rocks at the
windows of creativity / and how beautiful the
wreckage looks cascading through the air / you must
recognize that they gave me an audience / the ability
to stand on top of grief and sing with my entire chest /
I may be sorry about my heart / how it made a mess of
itself so grossly / publicly / but I'm not sorry for
writing about what happened / the art I forge from
heartache is just as valid / as what I'm able to squeeze
from joy / with the same hands

there isn't
space for you
in my life
anymore.

i have filled
all the
emptiness
with
forgiveness.

IMPRINT

I didn't realize that you'd accidentally taught me
how to do everything with my non-dominant hand
until I moved in with a lover and he watched me rip
a piece of foil.

Later, after the leftovers were wrapped and placed in
the refrigerator, I sat beside the photo albums and
wept.

You were here this whole time. Waiting in my muscle
memory for the right moment to say hello.

QUESTIONNAIRE

1. I put the same songs on every playlist I make. What does this say about me?
    a) I attach myself to beautiful things and cannot let go.
    b) My heart isn't big enough for everything I love to live there at all times.
    c) It says nothing. I just make everything into a metaphor.
    d) All of the above.

2. How often do you have control of your life?
    a) Whenever I write.
    b) Whenever I take care of my body on my own terms.
    c) Whenever I fall asleep within ten minutes of getting into bed.
    d) Never.

3. Where do you carry your grief?
    a) In the form of a question.
    b) To the nearest river.
    c) On my lower back.
    d) I don't.

4. You are worried about something. It's eating away at your chest, like moths to an old shirt. Who do you call?
    a) Someone you are related to by blood alone.
    b) Your reflection.
    c) Another living being, one that you love deeply despite knowing them for less than a decade.
    d) Home.

5. Which definition for vulnerability appeals to you the most?

a) Being exposed to the potential for physical or emotional harm.

b) Trusting that your environment will be kind if you are honest with it.

c) A necessary act in order to explore all areas of your own self.

d) A first kiss, not technically romantic but romantic enough to remember.

6. Why did you forgive them?

a) It was the only way to stop the dreams.

b) Time came to me in a vision.

c) The situation no longer made me cry in the shower.

d) They forgave me first.

7. What color is anger?

a) Your father's shirt.

b) Vodka.

c) Ripe fruit.

d) Dawn.

8. Which of these scenarios best illustrates your love language?

a) My partner knew that I needed to stop at the grocery store after work, and did it for me so I could come home and relax instead.

b) My partner saw that I was upset and held me close to them, close enough that our heartbeats fused into one singular hum, like a bee.

c) My partner constantly reminds me that I am worthy of love, and stability.

d) My partner stays.

9. How much space have you created between yourself and your regrets?
    a) At least one year's distance.
    b) An arm's length.
    c) I am my regrets.
    d) I no longer believe that I have done anything worth agonizing over.

10. When did you first find yourself drawn to the light?
    a) I have always been drawn to the light.
    b) a.
    c) b.
    d) c.

BRIEF SELF PORTRAIT AS FRANKENSTEIN'S MONSTER

You may have given me this tough skin,
a hand outstretched, a lifetime of words, but

how much do you have to despise what you've made
in order to leave it nameless?

SHORT REFLECTIONS ON GRIEF

There are so many stories that walk in a circle.
Endings and beginnings traipse barefoot through the
same rooms.

It's true that I kept the bedroom door unlocked for
Grief.
Didn't have the heart to move when it slid under the
bedsheets and wrapped me in its arms.

We talked into the dew-soaked dawn, almost tenderly.
There, in the graveyard of my mind, we mourned
everything I ruined before knowing better, wrote
obituaries to my memories and sent them into
the trees. We would fall asleep face to face, inhaling and
exhaling the same tired breath of air between us.

Upon waking I practiced drawing parallel lines,
hoping to set boundaries between my body and my
heartache.
To curate a space that was mine not knowing it had
only ever belonged to me.

I kept that, at the very least.
I nearly killed myself trying to burn it all down but I
kept the house I loved her in.

I grip the rage, the absence, tightly in my fists.
I let it go.

I let it go.
I grip the rage, the absence, tightly in my fists.

I nearly killed myself trying to burn it all down but I
kept the house I loved her in.
I kept that, at the very least.

To curate a space that was mine not knowing it had
only ever belonged to me.
Upon waking I practiced drawing parallel lines,
hoping to set boundaries between my body and my
heartache.

We would fall asleep face to face, inhaling and
exhaling the same tired breath of air between us.
There, in the graveyard of my mind, we mourned
everything I ruined before knowing better, wrote
obituaries to my memories and sent them into the
trees. We talked into the dew-soaked dawn, almost
tenderly.

Didn't have the heart to move when it slid under the
bedsheets and wrapped me in its arms.
It's true that I kept the bedroom door unlocked for
Grief.

Endings and beginnings traipse barefoot through the
same rooms.
There are so many stories that walk in a circle.

DEPRESSION, REVISITED

Sadness isn't the sharp shooting pain it once was.
Now it takes me out to dinner first.
Smoothes down my hair.
Waits until nightfall and swallows me whole.

HALF-CONDITIONAL STATEMENTS

if you have stood on the precipice of anger and let it
wash over you like sickness   if you have unhinged a
fishhook from a yellow perch just to throw it back into
a life of green   if you have waited for
somebody gentle to cajole you into happiness
if you have thrust your heart into the mouth of a cave
and listened for its echo   if you have survived
every past version of yourself   if you have used a
lighter for anything other than warmth   if you
have scratched a mosquito bite through your jeans
if you have been moved to tears by something unliving
          if you have remained stagnant longer than
you should've   if you have attempted to cut
mistakes out of your hair   if you have
untangled a jewelry drawer full of beads   if
you have craved physical attention so desperately that
it ruined your tongue   if you have shined a
flashlight onto grief   if you have dreamt of living
among the lonely   if your eyes have swept over a
crime scene and lingered   if you have felt
illuminated by loss   if you have burned a
hole through your idea of love and built something
sturdy and ephemeral in its absence   then be
comforted knowing that you are
still alive.

reminders

it is not
a crime
to be
difficult
to love

you will
never be
content
until you
rid
yourself
of the
desire to
be needed

being alone is
not a pit-stop
on the road to
romance

it is its own
destination

DISMEMBERED/AMBIGUOUS DREAM SEQUENCE

In the dream where parts of our bodies keep vanishing
I draw the curtains to let in more light while you stare
at your knee that's slowly becoming the absence
of a knee. In the dream I can name everything that's
missing but cannot visualize it. In the dream you
forget. In the dream I remember, which is very
undreamlike.
Dreams have no memory unless you give them one,
much like children or hospital rooms.

In the dream we only live one day at a time, 24
seamless hours of showering without a throat or
driving without ankles. In the dream we are always
together.
In the dream you always have your hands. In the
dream there is no past or future there is just now and
the knowledge that none of this is built to last. Not
even your soft belly. Not even your soft heart.

In the dream you are a combination of all the faces
I've ever known. In the dream you are my
grandmother and my last love and my first love and
the waitress in Niagara Falls that knew how I liked my
egg and cheese sandwich. You are the friends I lost at
18, the friends I carried through adolescence. You are
the man that sold me my car and the librarians that
recommended books about creativity. You are the
doctor. You are a machine.

In the dream you are incomplete and it doesn't bring
me to tears, though I can remember how it felt when
you were whole. The sound of a balloon popping, air
reclaiming what was always its own.

In the dream I asked, once, what the metaphor was
supposed to be and you tried to shrug, forgetting that
your shoulders had become the opposite of real.

Even now, years later, your presence an answering
machine blinking red into the night, I can't for the life
of me figure it out.

23

He'd been alive for four years by the time I was born
and I thought that made him all-knowing. I would
look at him as he snored and consider his shame,
fantasize about shoving it in my mouth, holding the sour
in my jaw until it ached, until I walked away with a
          cavity.

This August I embraced my birthday and kissed its
tender forehead. 23 has since held good years
with careful hands. Does not ask of me what it once
asked of him.

Now that the odds are balanced, our experience equal
as far as time is concerned, I can say with confidence
that he tried. He tried his best but even so,

I would never do to a girl in love what he did to me.

I AM BARELY HOLDING IT TOGETHER

and that gives me joy.

it implies that, at one point, I had it all together. it was
there, a full life for the ripening.

I AM BARELY HOLDING IT TOGETHER
and still take out my phone to type this into the notes
app like it'll find me a therapist or give me a
prescription. where does a life go when you place it
on hold? why have i, historically, held more space for
sadness than healing, or forgiveness?

I AM BARELY HOLDING IT TOGETHER
but, miraculously, i'm whole. and i don't know what
this says about the nonlinear nature of growth or
whether i'm doing a good job at maintaining
the world i've cultivated despite mental illness
but maybe not everything needs to mean something.
maybe i can have days where

I AM BARELY HOLDING IT TOGETHER
and focus on the fact that still, *still*,

I AM HOLDING IT TOGETHER.

BENJAMIN BUTTON

Another gray disappeared overnight.
My cheeks are berries, vibrant with survival.
Wrinkles tighten until the skin appears
smooth, ready to be laughed into creases.
These joints are flexible, splayed across
couch cushions. Scars waver
between there and not there like mirages.

Resurrection bargains with my body,
gives back the years I lost to grief and there are
many. Both years and bodies.

I'll never be older than I was at 19.

I CAN'T WATCH WOMEN DIE IN MOVIES ANYMORE

Scene One
I grew up with Dateline and the waxing gibbous and
my grandmother. Learned early on that it's the lovers
you need to dust for fingerprints. There were months
where Dolly and I watched Nancy Grace until the
backs of our eyelids felt like swimming pools of
battery acid, reflecting the murders we discussed over
sundaes and night lights. Back then we slept with our
doors open, creating a maw that yawned into static,
rupturing the silence. The dark was more than enough
privacy. I didn't need to be wrapped up, locked into it.
All I'm saying is that I used to fall asleep to CSI
Miami, we binge-watched Law and Order SVU, and
now whenever I see a woman onscreen, sobbing into
carpet, losing her self, I have to look away. My fear is
a cold case that refuses solving, pressing against my
tongue like a word I can no longer remember. And, of
course, empathy has swollen to overtake my life,
triggered by grief after grief unbearable. I can feel it,
the men and their red hands, gripping my legs,
holding a blade to the soft parts.

Scene Two
Anxiety is a Wikipedia page with hundreds of
sources, a list of victims that I read one by one,
savoring the syllables, honoring their names. I've
stared into the computer-screen eyes of a killer and
convinced myself that I could do it. I could point to

the most charismatic person you've ever met and tell you where he buries his ghosts. The exact words he said to get them there. I could tell you everything and still make the wrong decision.

Scene Three

Dolly and I would call across the hall to one another about who we thought *did it*. We examined the clues, the crime scenes, the predictable twists and herrings. She told me once that if she had the chance to redo her life she'd go into forensic science. She said *I'd love to work in the labs, analyze the data*. Soon after this confession, our show fading into temporary resolution, her breath grew deeper and lazier, drifting towards the bright face of her television. My brave and unfazed grandmother — unable to fall asleep without canned sitcom laughter in the background. If only she'd known how fearless she was. Can forensics determine why I only began cringing at the violence once she was dead? Why I can't predict any endings without her?

Scene Four

The evidence my body committed to muscle memory now aches in tandem with my loneliness. When I'm handed the blindfold, reeking with her perfume, I say thank you. I tie the knot myself.

ANOTHER POEM ABOUT GRIEF, BUT NOW IT OWNS PROPERTY

grief has always kept a neat house, which is to say
sometimes feelings are so large that there
isn't space for anything else.

sometimes you need to rethink the decorative wall art
or the wooden coffee tables because as soon as grief
walks into the room it'll all shatter into
nothing.

the last time i shattered into
nothing
the backseat of my car became a room and i became a
locked door, a disembodied hand jiggling the knob
as if to turn it into an answer.

grief sleeps in its bathtub and calls it baptism.

grief watches the drain tug cold water into its depths
and daydreams about shattering into
nothing
so i remind her that shattering into
nothing
is just another way to make a maze out of your body.
i say *have you seen the shining? it's kinda like that.*
and she says
nothing,
either because she doesn't understand the reference
or she doesn't want to think about its implications.

grief keeps every letter she's ever received under the
sink. there's one, crumpled and nearly forgotten, at
the bottom, from the person i was at 19.

a brief, unanswered note in a plain envelope
asking if grief has any available beds for a visitor.

WHAT WE TALK ABOUT WHEN WE TALK ABOUT VINCENT VAN GOGH

Not the passion that overtook him
or the words that flew from his hands like birds.
Not the final letter he drafted to his brother, writing
"I still love art and life very much," before going out
to paint. Not the obstacles that prevented creation
at the level he desired. Not what could've been.
Not the reality. Not the love he had for small
pleasures and graceful things. Not that his most
iconic work was made in recovery. Not the full
picture, nowhere near the full picture. An edited
approximation.

EVERYTHING
I'VE WRITTEN
ABOUT YOU IS
STILL ABOUT
ME

ODE FOR THE GIRLS THAT CAMP OUT FOR CONCERTS

this is for the dirt-stained beauty queen street sleepers
made of resilience and dollar store glitter. the girls
that can turn a half-empty bag of makeup wipes into a
full body shower. the girls that keep buying the
cheapest item on the local fast food menu so they can
use their bathroom. the girls that pray to dry shampoo
and deodorant, spray it generously over anyone that
needs it. the girls that make friends with security &
tell them about their parents, how they don't know
that they're here, curled up on a sidewalk. how they
think they're at a sleepover with a friend from high
school that isn't actually their friend anymore,
watching movies, gossiping about nothing. the girls
applying eyeshadow in the reflections of storefront
windows, unfazed by every person that walks past and
dares to roll their eyes. there is something holy about
girls so dedicated to melody that they give up their
basic needs for it. live off of bottled water and bulk-
sized bags of goldfish crackers just for the chance to
touch something intangible. to show off tattoos they
got while holding hands with one another, screaming
the words to a song that saved their life or makes them
happy or maybe just reminds them of how beautiful it
is to be alive, how absolutely wonderful it is to sing in
a crowd that knows every key change by heart. the
girls that have only ever been a part of something
bigger than themselves. the girls that wave pride flags
and kiss their partners and hand out hair ties like

they're compliments. the girls that trade water with strangers, lips to lips to lips, trusting that everyone here is safe because they are, they have to be, how else would they have gotten through the door? why else would they have sweat through their tee shirts or shivered through their jeans, borrowed their uncle's old tent and stretched out on blankets that have seen better days? why else if it isn't some sort of untouchable magic, a silent understanding that everybody belongs in this collective space? this is for the girls that look discomfort in the face until it backs away in shame. the girls that tuck portable phone chargers in their back pockets and memorize setlists. the girls with ripped band shirts and flower crowns. the girls waking up the next morning at 6am for reality. the girls without a family that understands the weird mix of heartbreak and joy they're capable of holding in their hands. the girls that believe.

you are heard. you are seen. you are here to stay.

LOVE POEM FOR PAUL

I love you like reading outdoors in late July.
I love you like fireworks against black skies, how
if you close your eyes they stay there for just a few
seconds longer.
I love you like moths wanting the porch light, getting
it, and then not landing on it because they're
too excited to enjoy it.
I love you like getting caught in the rain
when there's an umbrella under your arm.
I love you like waiting for our downstairs neighbor to
leave so we can dance to Glenn Miller on your record
player, because my cousin's wedding is soon and if I
stepped on you in heels it would probably hurt.
I love you like washing our clothes in the same load
of laundry.
I love you like the squeal of my rusty brakes piercing
the slow morning air.
I love you like the birds in Delmar sing.
I love you like the Kit Kat bar in the refrigerator that
you brought home because I'm on my period.
I love you like a full refrigerator.
I love you like an ice cube, clinking against
a sweaty glass.
I love you like the day before my birthday.
I love you like Halloween.
I love you like every stupid cliché that's ever been
written and overused and plagiarized.
Most of all, if I had to pick a favorite,

I love you like waking up every morning and getting to kiss your warm, kind face.
Knowing with certainty that neither of us are going anywhere.

IPHONE NOTES
7:14 AM

We are quotation marks jammed up against one
another, the beginning to a poem I haven't written

yet.

AFTER

After you left I realized there were so many things
I'd never know.
The sound of your younger feet walking
on linoleum, the feel of a Harley, the color of your
natural hair at 77, the smell of your house before I
filled it with mine.

I had to mourn a history I'd never bothered to write
down, family names that died with your mouth.

After you left it occurred to me that I never pictured
you leaving.
I thought time would wait until I was old enough to
negotiate.

After you left I began to love someone with a kind
heart. Someone that held hands with me in the
Niagara Falls state park and taught me how to slow
dance with vinyl records and peach wine.

I'd never thought sleeping across the hall from you
was a luxury until our conversations moved to the
cemetery or, more often, my car, at dusk.

Over a year after you left
I was still singing grievances, had to acknowledge that
you'll never be able to meet him, my best love, my
final love.

Can you forgive my selfishness?
How far away I wandered when the doctor said you
weren't coming back?

After you left there was only one thing I could
remember how to do. Here I am, doing it now.
It was the only way I knew I could talk to you.

After you left, three years after you left, I finally told
the page *I think I know who I am.*

And for a moment it felt like providence.

I SAID YOUR NAME THREE TIMES IN THE MIRROR

begging for a haunting, but all I saw was my own
reflection. So, maybe I'm the ghost. It's been three
years and I'm still finding new things to say about
this. I wanted a haunting because that has to be better
than silence. This wound of living. I'll throw the
plates myself if you just give me some goosebumps.
I'm desperate for contact and a desperate woman
never wants the right things. How do I break a mirror?
A promise? When the world is shutting down who's
left to sell me a Ouija board? It didn't always feel this
difficult. I didn't always need to talk to you before
leaving the house. What am I supposed to say? I'm
sad. I miss you, and is it so wrong that I do? After all
of the space we converted into memory? I'm getting
off track. I'm a ghost. Let's say that I'm the ghost.
Now say my name, I can't remember how it sounded
coming from your mouth. It feels like I have so little
to look back to. Fewer moments than hands are able to
hold. The point is that one of us is dead and it doesn't
matter anymore which is which.
It just doesn't matter.

I WAS ONCE A FIST
IN THE PROCESS OF
UNCLENCHING.

NOW I AM THE AIR
AROUND IT.

EVIDENCE SUGGESTING MY DOWNSTAIRS NEIGHBOR IS TERRIBLY LONELY

She shouts on the phone for hours, filling our
apartments with inescapable background noise.
When she puts the speaker on full volume, she can
close her eyes and almost imagine the other line
is sitting beside her.
She's never been alone like this before,
isn't sure how to lie in bed without accommodating
a man's torso. I have to assume the walls are choked
by framed photographs, given her incessant pounding
on them at all hours. Unsteady nails hammered
with unsure hands, taken down by the slightest
whisper, the weakest sigh.
My downstairs neighbor has spent her life twisting
loose ends into place, insisting that they were never
broken to begin with. They always belonged to her.

I imagine that she's heard my love and me, before.
These walls are thinner than my patience. I imagine
she's heard us try to quote *Dirty Dancing* in front of
the television, squeals when he sneaks up behind me
mid-dishes, bombarding my neck with kisses. Our
singing, our footsteps rushing towards one another,
his steady voice as he teaches me
the best way to light a match and peel a boiled egg.
All reminders of what she lost, and how long it's been
since she lost it.

It makes sense that she'd feel bitter with that sort of

affection constantly hanging over her head. No wonder she feels the need to cry into these early spring nights for somebody, anybody, to listen, just listen, please, for thirty seconds, to her voice. I suppose I'd also feel desperate if I started to realize that the ruckus has just been a way to camouflage the silence, the oppressive and suffocating absence.

I suppose, then, I'd finally hear the quiet, in all its unflinching, awful honesty, and be frightened by it, too.

1234

the slice of fresh mozzarella you
bring me from the kitchen
in the middle of preparing our dinner
crumbles on my tongue like a sigh of relief.

in the quiet hours of our lives
you have reinvented love for me.

I DIDN'T WANT TO CRY OVER THIS

but you always ask me to cut the onions
and I always do, because I love you.

It was December, the first time I witnessed tears
bubble over your eyelashes.
We were handmaking pierogies, vegetables scattered
across the countertop, and I was thinking about
tradition. How every holiday moving forward
I want something to call ours.

I didn't have a family that pushed dough between
fingertips, neither of us had one that chose eternity
but to hell with all that.
I look at you and think this is *it*.
This is it for me.

A warm house that smells like desire.
Your voice, waltzing with steam in the kitchen.

My hand steady on the knife, all tender and no hurt.

BLUE SKY LOVE, I SING YOU HAPPY

I know you like I know music, like I know the melody
that arrives in my chest when I'm lost within the
noise. The moments between us when speech is
inconceivable have filled me like a balloon — I could
float forever on the songs we've left to reflex.

If I'd known that the smoke of heartache led to you
I would've put on running shoes and barreled through
it headfirst. Dipped into the well of youth and put out
the fire instead of taking a year to warm my hands in
it. Sometimes I love you so much that it spills
out of my mouth and onto the floor like an oil slick,
our reflection dancing in the blackness like a dream.

Lately I've been clutching "this time" to my chest like
a blessing. "This time" I won't throw a rug over the
marks on the floor. "This time" it'll be remarkable in
its simplicity. Like the sound of our bedroom door
groaning its way into openness. The knowledge
that you've come back to bed to kiss me goodbye.

Oh, how I think about kissing you.

About the taste of your breath, hot and alive.
Sometimes I want to swallow you whole, unhinge my
jaw and imagine a happiness that would ensure you'll
never leave me, that I'll never want you to go but how
could I? How could I when you're the reason I have

materials to build with?
Everything I've written for the past two years has
been about love, which means it's all been about you,
in some way, and what I've learned about love
is that I didn't know what the hell it looked like
until you picked it out of a crowd and introduced me.

I could write my hands to ruin and still never capture
the timbre of your laughter after midnight
or the way I cry in the shower over the hearts you've
drawn in the steam. I could dedicate every poem I
ever write to you and it wouldn't be enough.
It just wouldn't be enough to express the joy I've
experienced through being loved well by you.
By loving you so loudly that anyone who has a
conversation with me leaves knowing your name.

When I tell you that I love you I mean
I have never once wondered what would happen if we
were to part. I have never planned for a future that
didn't include you.
When I tell you that I love you I mean
what I feel for you has made me consider
that every other time I've uttered those words
it's been a huge lie. That until I met you I didn't know
anything at all.

The truth is that I don't have anything of substance
to say. Nothing unique or worth repeating
just words on a page rushing
to a finish line

but you are the only person I always want
to say nothing to. I have loved you for my entire life.

ODE TO MELODRAMA

The blue-fingered midnights that once held me
together have faded into the minor details of my
history. Not forgotten, no, but remembered at a
distance. Once, I was nineteen and burning and
feeling everything at once. I didn't have language
for my body until it was given to me. When does bad
love begin to spoil? Driving home from the coffee
shop where I wrote his sins, past the street where we
kissed elbows and bargained with hours, the voice on
the radio called my heart a fossil. Timeworn and
valuable and known and understood. My GPS named
this place home for six months after it was over.
Sometimes I cried so hard that the windshield became
just another moving picture that looked too much like
my life.

The voice on the radio called my hurt a lot of things.
Sometimes *a liability*. Other times *hard feelings*.
Always it was *just another graceless night* letting go
of the little things. I healed to spite the art that told me
I could keep going, continue wringing the neck of my
breakup for every poem it was worth, until there was
nothing left of me but the supernatural past.
A boom in my chest.

It's true, yes, that I kept myself alive, fevered and
rosy-cheeked. But knowing someone else had
attempted it before me and succeeded, well — it was a
green light, shimmering noisily in the dark.

THE WOMAN I WAS

The woman I was at 19 cries in car washes
not because she's sad
but because sometimes it feels like the right thing to
do, like putting on lipstick to go to the supermarket
or waving goodbye until everything
is the back of your hand.
She wipes off her face when she spots daylight
at the tunnel's end, defines affection in terms of how
she's received it and not by what she herself
has given, which is to say that she does not define it
in a way that allows her to sleep at night.

She's timid,
believes with her chest that love is never going
to find her.
She isn't stupid,
she just hasn't come to terms with loss yet.
She doesn't know how to part with someone without
building them a commemorative statue.
Her hands remain a bloodied mess of thorn and
memory.

Years later, I recognize that the pressure
I placed on her to be healthy was anything but.
That the lonely methods she tried to heal by were not
chosen in ignorance but in hope that this, maybe,
finally, will work out. And of course none of them
did, but it wasn't her fault.

Ignorant isn't the worst thing a young person can be.

I step out of my body, unfold forgiveness, and hand it
to her, the woman I was at 19.
She smooths down the creases of the page and reads
this:

it's okay that you
spent ▓ so
much time
painting your-
self the
color of your
background.

you haven't
.<u>made</u> a <u>home</u>
in anything
that you
cannot shed
the skin of.

FOR ANYONE THAT KNEW ME INTIMATELY IN 2017

For a while, words were less of a luxury and more
of a lifeboat. I put baggage into a mouth that felt like
mine and mumbled around the edges of it.
Begged, and begged. I missed her. I missed him.
Love meant less than grief and grief I hardly
understood at all. And you listened, closely
and then not so closely and I don't blame you.
Everything I felt in 2017 was a different iteration of
the same rage. I wept on the eve of my youth with hot
tears and so much shame. It held me like I hold eggs
in the seconds before cracking. How I held my
stomach during the months where I was too anxious
to buy groceries.
And you told me to eat.
You drove me around the river and we listened
to Paramore. *Survival will not be the hardest part.*
You sent me letters. You read the book.
You bought a ticket.

Gratitude once overwhelmed me to the point of
silence but I don't lose balance when I talk about the
past anymore. I may waver, but I remain upright.
I was gone but I promise, I want to stay.

if you remember
anything about me,
i hope it is
how brave i became
in the aftermath.

43.0216° N, 78.9657° W

Usually my memory is more cloudy than not
but every street in my hometown is a bolt
of lightning, forcing me to remember.

The weathered stop signs lining the edges of my first
known world are like a guiding constellation, fiery
with names and faces
I no longer understand the intimacies of.

My car, relearning terrain I granted it a year
to forget, rolls over the tired asphalt where I once held
a white sparkler like an extension of my heart.

Past the sidewalk where I skinned my right knee
trying to catch an ice cream truck that never stopped.

Around Fisherman Landing where Sarah and I would
listen to The Smiths and unpack our grief.

It's a subtle joy to know
where every pothole lives on a stretch of road.
To know that love is bound to familiarity with yards
and yards of barbed wire.
Oh, the truth is I hated living here until I wasn't living
here.

Now nostalgia complicates my steering patterns.

I don't require anything more than an alphabet to
catapult out of my birthplace
but that doesn't mean I'm not afraid of its hands.

With just enough time and the right amount of
gentleness I think I could forget everything
that drove me away in the first place.

I think I could accidentally forgive it all.

THE SURRENDER THEORY PART II

My heart crawls into bed and asks for advice.
Its ankles are swollen with devotion. There isn't
anywhere safe to put them down.

If I were younger I would pull the quilt around my
torso, curl my feet into the backs of my thighs.
But grief has taught me a lot about surrender.
I choose to stand in front of the years that ridiculed
my tenderness.

My heart is less creature and more trying her best.
Less sacrifice. More empathy.

I say, don't bleed for anything that doesn't stay with
you until morning.

I say, I have no interest in dying for the things I love
anymore.

It's better just to live for them.

BLESS
EVERY
PERSON
I
HAD
TO
BE
BEFORE
I
COULD
BE
THIS
ONE

MY GRANDMOTHER STANDS AT THE END OF THE DRIVEWAY, 2011

after Lyd Havens

Birdseed falls from her hand like rose petals
in a haphazard line connecting the left side of the yard
to the right. If she were to drive anywhere
her Chevy Cruze would roll right over it,
unintentionally plant the seeds into the ground.
A group of pigeons have claimed the abandoned
building across from us and she's named them
1, 2, 3, and 4. We identify them by how comfortable
they are with our shared presence. 2 will fly up to us
before we've even emptied the bag.
3 waits until we're on the couch, binoculars in hand.
It was with dusty hands that I began to love the coo
of a pigeon, the innocence of its demands.
The dilapidated bones that served as their watchtower
was once a car dealership, owned by my
grandmother's father, my great grandfather.
Alt Chevrolet. The birds had left by the time I realized
that "Alt" was not the Chevrolet company's first,
omitted, name, but rather something that every
dealership owner did to mark their territory. I thought
every car with a bowtie on its back-end
rightfully belonged to me. To her.
In photographs of myself, waiting at the bus stop with
a Powerpuff Girls backpack, you can see the cars
parked in neat lines behind me, like
an image dragged across a computer screen
or tire marks on a street, remnants of a driver

bargaining with their brakes.

My grandmother was still alive when they began
building storage units in the place where her father
once sold movement, many years after I found out that
I wasn't a secret Chevy Heiress.

She said *it could be worse* which might be
one of the saddest sentences I know.

Memory does not allow me the gift of gradualism.

One day everything is there — the vehicles shiny and
stickered, four pigeons babbling in the driveway, my
grandmother with half of her hair in a pink scrunchie,
small and kind, refusing to name the creatures she
feeds — and by morning,

bathed in gold and needy light,

it's gone.

NASA DIDN'T FIND A PARALLEL UNIVERSE WHERE TIME RUNS BACKWARDS

but, for a moment, I allow myself to believe they did.
My clean birth in a king-sized bed followed, decades
later, by a swift death, sliding heels first into a full
stomach, screaming the entire way down. Like a
calendar on a wall I carry my history
with a thumbtack through the heart,
shoulder the weight of each moment until I set it down
and never pick it up again.
In this universe I leave with nothing, not even a
memory. I am sick with not knowing.

We aren't so different, my parallel universe self and I.
Our love pouring from the faucet before it's sucked
back up. Our poems erasing themselves line by line
into blank pages and then into trees, branches severing
the blue sky like a knife. This is the price you pay for
writing a life — you must play witness to a wound
sealing itself up, just to be reopened with a
ballpoint pen.

When I blink for the first time, inhale my first breath,
there aren't many things I can say with utmost
certainty, but I know this much is true:
I have a voice that sings louder than grief. So I do.

NOTES

"Lies" was written after Yena Sharma Purmasir's "Things That Aren't True," published in *[Dis]Connected: Poems & Stories of Connection and Otherwise*.

"Possible Titles For Future Breakup Poems" references lyrics from "September" by Earth, Wind & Fire.

"I Reenact 'The Last Five Years' In My Kitchen Instead Of Going To Therapy" refers to the musical by Jason Robert Brown, and borrows both characters and imagery from it.

"Nick Carraway Wakes In The Middle Of The Night And Reaches For A Pen" refers to a character from *The Great Gatsby* by F. Scott Fitzgerald, and borrows imagery from that novel. "Benjamin Button" also borrows its title from a Fitzgerald character.

"Nesting Doll" had a wonderful home prior to this one, with *Rust + Moth*.

"Numb Recollections" has italicized lyrics from the song "Can't Feel My Face" by The Weeknd.

"Anxiety As Inheritance" was written after ideas explored in Søren Kierkegaard's *The Concept Of Anxiety*.

"Saying Your Names" was written after Richard Siken's poem of the same name, in his collection *Crush*.

"The Artist Paints A Favorable Portrait of Jack Torrance" and "Wendy Torrance Practices Revisionist History" both borrow characters, themes, and images from Stephen King's *The Shining*.

"The Anxiety Speaks" was written after "The Mania Speaks" by Jeanann Verlee.

"Dolly Cries During The Movie" refers to *The Bridges Of Madison County* (1995).

"Penelope" borrows images from Homer's *The Odyssey*.

"Self Portrait As Frankenstein's Monster" was inspired by Mary Shelley's *Frankenstein*.

"Blue Sky Love, I Sing You Happy" plays with ideas about love letters by Roland Barthes, articulated in his book *A Lover's Discourse*.

"Ode To Melodrama" refers to and references songs from Lorde's album *Melodrama*.

"For Anyone That Knew Me Intimately In 2017" has italicized lyrics from "26" by Paramore.

"My Grandmother Stands At The End Of The Driveway, 2011" was deeply inspired by Lyd Havens's poem "My Grandmother, In Maine At Dawn" in their book *Chokecherry*.

ACKNOWLEDGMENTS

I'd like to thank Michelle and the Central Avenue team for believing in me and the work that I do. To hold a book of my poems has been a dream for as long as I've been a dreamer, and you made that possible for me.

Many of the poems in this book were born and refined in creative writing workshops. Some of these include a wonderful poetry course with Karen Mac Cormack taken at the University at Buffalo, the 2018 "Catalyze Self-Revolution" Poets House workshop run by Winter Tangerine, and the Slumber Party Retreat hosted by Sabrina Benaim and Clementine von Radics. I'm incredibly grateful to all of these instructors and the folks in these courses for holding space for me.

Trista Mateer, I wouldn't be the poet that I am if it weren't for you. Thank you for your advice and guidance. For being honest when I ask you how to make a poem better. For introducing me to so many incredible people. For listening to my voice memos even when they get long and rambly (which they often do). Etc.

Thank you to the poets I've written casually with, via Zoom and otherwise, in the past couple of years. When there weren't any workshops or retreats being offered, you provided that for me in brilliant technicolor. You know who you are.

Paul — thank you for everything. Absolutely everything I could possibly thank a person for. I love you.

&, of course, Dolly. I hope you don't mind being on the cover of this book. I miss you in the strangest places.

Caitlin Conlon is a poet and avid reader who lives in upstate New York. She has a BA in English and a Creative Writing Certificate from the University at Buffalo and, while there, was chosen for the Friends of the University Libraries Undergraduate Poetry Prize, and the Arthur Axlerod Memorial Prize for Poetry. Caitlin has previously been published via *Up The Staircase Quarterly* and *Rust + Moth*, among others. *The Surrender Theory* is her first collection of poetry.

You can find her online almost anywhere at @cgcpoems.

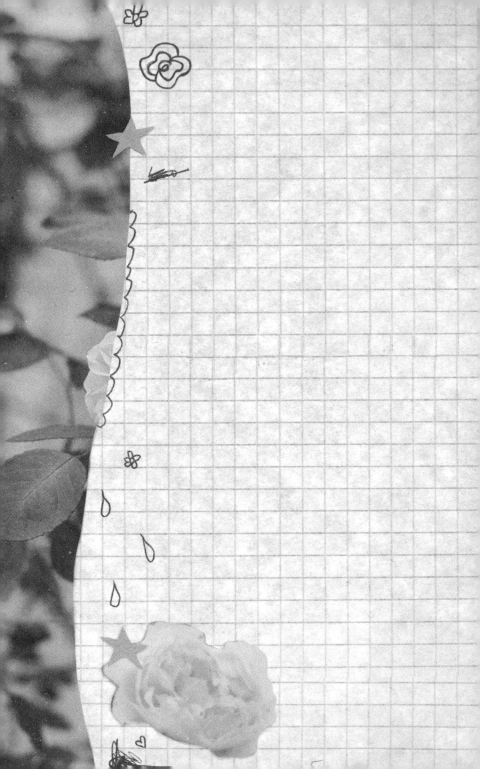